A Cry for Mercy

A Cry for
Mercy

William Cawley

ARCHWAY
PUBLISHING

Archway Publishing books may be ordered through booksellers or by contacting:

Archway Publishing
1663 Liberty Drive
Bloomington, IN 47403
www.archwaypublishing.com
1 (888) 242-5904

RSV-CE: The Catholic Edition of the Revised Standard Version of the
Bible, copyright 1965, 1966 by the Division of Christian Education
of the National Council of the Churches of Christ in the United
States of America. Used by permission. All rights reserved.

ISBN: 978-1-4808-6990-5 (sc)
ISBN: 978-1-4808-6991-2 (e)

Library of Congress Control Number: 2018912447

Print information available on the last page.

Archway Publishing rev. date: 11/9/2018

To
The Blessed Mother, St. Francis of Assisi,
St. Padre Pio, St. Mother Teresa,
my wife Teresa,
my daughter Kristina,
my greatest teacher Ann,
and my spiritual directors,
most
especially
Fr. Rock Travnikar
and
Msgr. John McNulty,
whose
holiness
allowed me
proximity to Christ.

Contents

Father in Heaven

I've written this book as a response to the love You've given me for Your church and Your people. I acknowledge that I am a sinner, which I know clouds my seeing. The plank in my eye is large indeed, yet I know You see all and bring forth good from all things. I pray, Father, that You bring good out of this smallest of efforts on my part to speak to our growing need for You. You have granted me the grace of experiencing this deep need in my own life, and it has helped me to see and experience how far from You I am. I do not want to be judged and want to rely completely on Your mercy, so please help me to avoid any judgment of my brothers and sisters and to offer these observations and experiences from the depth of Your love. I want only to be united to Your will and write this book with the hopes that in so doing I may be of service to that which is yet lacking in Your body, of which I lack the most. Therefore, I cry out, "Lord, have mercy on me, a sinner!"

Bless the people who read this book. Help them as You would help me to believe in You, to humble ourselves before You, and to realize our need for You. Then together may we cry out, "Mercy, Lord. Have mercy on us." I also ask that You bless those who help correct my errors and my perspectives that I may better see You, know You, and serve You in what is remaining of my life.

With the sincerest of gratitude, I offer you praise.

Your unworthy servant,

William

Why a Cry for Mercy?

I read the scriptures and sense the deep mercy God wants to share with us, His constant reminders to turn from our sins, and His warnings as from the mouth of the prophet Amos: "'Behold, the days are coming,' says the Lord God, 'when I will send a famine on the land; not a famine of bread, nor a thirst for water, but of hearing the words of the Lord. They shall wander from sea to sea, and from north to east; they shall run back and forth, to seek the word of the Lord, but they shall not find it'" (Amos 8:11–12).[1] He reminds us that His justice is demanding, and He makes clear how we sin against Him and ourselves. I sense His deep love and His reluctance to punish us, but we don't listen.

Then I become so angry that there are few places to find love, mercy, and peace in this world—that everyone, it seems, including myself, is focused on themselves and acts with greed,

---

[1] All scripture references are taken from Ignatius Bible, revised standard ed. (2005).

pride, and lust. I've become acutely aware of my own failures, my past sins, and even now the remnants of sin that pull at me constantly. I don't want to sin or to offend God or my neighbor. I want to live in love and do God's will, and it seems that I'm constantly seeking the way in which I can serve, but I'm never sure that I am in fact doing so. Can anyone help me? Are there not spiritual leaders who can direct me, guide me, or correct me? Why doesn't my church hear me?

Why *A Cry for Mercy*? I think the church needs more saints, and I want to be one of them. I've come to believe that I cannot be a saint without your help. And while it seems to me that our world has never needed God more, it also seems like our church has never reflected God's mercy less. I fear we have reached a point in history where individuals reflect what God laments through the mouth of the prophet Jeremiah, and which is referenced again in Matthew 2:18: "A voice was heard in Ramah, wailing and loud lamentation, Rachel weeping for her children; she refused to be consoled, because they were no more." In some translations, "no more" is translated as "dead."

Dead! Not just dying but dead already. Are we dead? Is our church dead to us?

Why do I care? Why should you? What does a line written two thousand years ago, even one with such a stark and somber message as this, have to do with any of us? I think the true answer is everything and more. Are we willing to hear the message?

In a way, this is a story of a troubled heart—namely mine. I often experience God's grace, and I see it in the lives of those around me. But I also find that each of us is struggling in our own ways, and we often fail to meet our own expectations—let alone those of the world around us. I want to say right up front that I haven't found some magical solution, and I can't promise you that the challenges facing you will be diminished, but I do want you to consider that God is sustaining us and offering us a lighter yoke. In fact, more than that, He provides a joy that is ever present, and He encourages us to hear the call of His loving voice. God holds us in the palm of His hand. He whispers to us to come and "learn from me, for I am gentle and lowly in heart, and you will find rest for your souls" (Matthew 11:29). He won't let go. Like the hound of heaven, He seeks us relentlessly. So, recognizing that He isn't going to give up on us, let us finally stop and turn to Him. Let us finally surrender to His love and respond more willingly.

Each of us has our own unique story of God in our lives. My awareness of my relationship with God started early. I remember being only four years old when I had my first sincere conversation with my mother on the subject of good and evil. I was sitting in a chair that you had to pass when moving from one room to another. It was a typical morning in our house, and therefore there was some hubbub going on somewhere. I found myself in a rare reflective moment, observing everything around me. I noticed the light coming in from the window and the stillness of the room. My mother had just walked past me a second time without noticing me seated quietly in the corner chair. She was preoccupied with my siblings' misbehavior. I was generally an obedient child and did not cause much trouble for my mother. As a mother of seven, she had much on her mind and in her hands. However, it struck me how my behaving meant that I did not receive attention. So naturally, I started to misbehave. A few hours later, my mother, exasperated, sat me down and asked me what was wrong. She commented that it was not like me to be so misbehaved and wanted to know why. I told her of my feeling invisible as she attended to my siblings and that I had misbehaved to get her attention. She hugged me and told me that I was her little angel and that she was sorry. She said that she certainly didn't mean to neglect me and would be extra careful not to ignore me in the future. In this interaction, I saw for the first time how I used evil to get what I wanted. I also saw the exasperation on the face of a loving mother who realized she had failed the needs of her son. I think in that encounter we both grew in our understanding of our limitations.

As a boy, like so many boys, I wanted the respect of my father, but even more so I wanted the love of my mother. She often called me her little angel, and I felt loved and safe in her arms. My mother had a great trust in God, and she shared that faith through the example of her life. As you can tell from the story of a four-year-old, my mother was loving and kind and attentive to the needs of her children. This compassion extended to others as well. No one was unwelcome at our house; although we were nine in all, my mother opened our home to those in need. Over the years, this would include alcoholics and children whose home lives were even more difficult than ours. She taught us to pray the rosary and, although she bore the worst of them, to overlook the sins of our father. My father was a hard man with high expectations and little tolerance. He demanded honesty and obedience, and he valued intellect above all else. Our Catholic faith was to be studied, the priests and the sisters were to be obeyed, and we were to participate in regular confession and attendance at Mass. Faith and religion were for him a militaristic discipline.

The contrast between my mother's tenderness and compassion and my father's strict observance meant that my relationship with God and the Roman Catholic Church was one of both love and fear. This dichotomy has led me to say on many occasions that I got my faith from my mother and my religion from my father. I attended Catholic school, weekly Mass, and frequent confession. My mother helped me find opportunities to assist at the convent. I paid attention and studied. I liked the sisters and school. I also liked to help when called upon. Perhaps this was due to wanting to emulate my older sister Kathy, who was always volunteering. More likely it was a way of gaining favor with my father, which in turn might help me to avoid his terrible anger.

I did well in school and responded to my father's claim that I should study hard, work hard, and apply myself and my intelligence to be successful in this world. I bought into the American dream, told God to get behind me, and went for it. For a while, I felt successful, at least as our culture defined it—big house, new car, nice clothes, and vacations at the beach. I started my own company. Then suddenly my luck turned, and I experienced economic crash, illness, deaths of family members, and a different relationship with the church. I found myself lost. I turned back to God and found myself wanting to feed the poor, clothe the naked, and visit those in prison—but I couldn't, and I was beginning to sense that none of us can do these things by ourselves. Only with God, when we remain in Him through His church, can we fulfill or even contribute to His mission. God needs us as well to give Him our five loaves and two fish to work together, believe, and put our love of neighbor in action. I've since served as a Eucharist minister and a Respect Life leader, and today I serve as a sponsor and catechist in the RCIA process. I believe that in some way God has provided me a glimpse of His love and grace through walking with those who have committed their hearts to Him. Wanting to come closer to God has me reflecting on the church we experience today. I find many who are seeking but even more who seem to have lost hope. They no longer even pretend to believe. In fact, having placed their faith in consumerism and our progressive values and finding themselves especially wanting, they seem even more than lost. They seem abandoned to me—and abandoned by our church, who is supposed to be mother to all.

We know that children who receive no response to their cries eventually stop crying. They no longer expect their needs to be met. The result is that they will languish in their current state of need until that which is uncared for brings them to a bitter end. Far too many of the people of God found in the pews and those who have given up attending religious services altogether have reached the point of no expectation. It appears that God has abandoned them just as they have abandoned God. In this case, the parables of the lost coin and the lost sheep come to mind. In these parables, Jesus reminds us that it is possible for the church to neglect her children. We as a church are failing to bring God's mercy to the people. Perhaps like the children, many of us have stopped crying because we no longer expect our church to meet our needs, or, even more disconcerting, we no longer expect our God to hear us. Yet I cannot help but share with you the depth of the ache in my own heart, the tears that stream down my face so regularly that I am in a constant state of suffering. These experiences convince me that there may still be time. And so, I cry out. This book is my cry for mercy, unable to sit idly hoping that we will wake up to what is happening to us.

I'm writing this book with the hope that in the expression of my own needs, you will be reminded of yours. My wish is that you too will cry out to our God, who is ever waiting for us to respond to his loving mercy. He has not forgotten us. God tells us in Psalm 34 that He is near to the brokenhearted and saves those who are crushed in spirit.

Let us cry again so loud that God Himself will hear us and send us shepherds who, like the pope, will walk with us and—by their proximity—come to smell like us, as the shepherd smells like his sheep. With this cry, we will be aided in our return to the Father.

I'm assuming that you still feel some absence in your hearts, some desire for something that you sense is lacking in this world, and that you are still open to exploring that sense. Perhaps you want to fill that gap with a lasting peace or, at a minimum, are willing to consider that what you've tried so far hasn't brought you the satisfaction you're seeking.

When I was in third grade, about eight years old, I had an experience of the church that has most certainly helped keep hope alive in my heart. My family was quite poor. In many ways, we were a typical Irish Catholic family—seven children, a recovering alcoholic father, poor but determined to do better. We attended Catholic school yet never paid tuition. With Easter approaching, my mother took my younger brother and sister and me to the rectory to pick up clothing to wear to Easter Mass. I vaguely recall trying a few things on, but what I do remember is that on the way home after Easter Mass, a friendly neighbor who was a photographer for the police department took a photo of all of us children in our Sunday best. I still treasure that photo and, reflecting on it, realize that I felt proud to have been wearing clothes in which I felt good about myself. The church had clothed us, and it made a difference in how I experienced my self-confidence, my faith, and my community. I miss that church. Over the years, I've experienced something very different on far too many occasions and more and more frequently.

The church today is a messy place and can be perceived as quite complex. With an honest reflection on our weaknesses and failures, we are reminded of the opportunity we have to invite God's grace into our lives to make us new again. I should note that in every area of weakness I point out, there are countless examples of the church doing just what it should, with the love of God as motivation. Many serve with Christ on their lips, love in their heart, and service from their hands. In fact, I would go so far as to say that the Catholic Church lives all of the beatitudes in this world more than any other single organization.

So then, what's the problem? A review of Revelations 3:1–6, an apocalyptic vision of the future, must offer us pause as we contemplate God's admonition:

> And to the angel of the church in Sardis write: "The words of him who has the seven spirits of God and the seven stars. 'I know your works; you have the name of being alive, and you are dead. Awake, and strengthen what remains and is on the point of death, for I have not found your works perfect in the sight of my God. Remember then what you received and heard; keep that, and repent. If you will not awake, I will come like a thief, and you will not know at what hour I will come upon you.'"

There are those who believe that having acted in God's name they would be saved, yet Jesus is quick to point out that "many will say … 'Lord, Lord, did we not prophesy in your name, and cast out demons in your name, and work many mighty works in your name?' and then Jesus will declare to them, 'I never knew you, Depart from me, you evildoers!'" (Mt 7:23). Are we so confident that these words are not addressed to us? Does our God find our "works complete"?

I Was Hungry, and You Ignored Me

Each month, the parish I attend holds a food collection for the poor. Parishioners place food at the back of the church to be collected for the Kaye Prox Food Bank. We're a parish of approximately three thousand registered families, and the latest information suggests we're growing by thirty families per month. Yet our total food collection wouldn't feed more than a hundred people. Twenty-six thousand people die of starvation or curable disease every day in the world. It's been estimated that the cost to eradicate this is $50 million a year. There are reportedly 1.1 billion Catholics on the planet. Less than five cents more a year from each Catholic could eradicate starvation. I recently mentioned these sobering statistics to a church leadership group and recommended a charity that will send twenty-five to thirty-one meals for every dollar donated. I was surprised at the pushback I received. "The poor will always be with us," was one response. Another member cited the complexity of the problem, and another indicated that we shouldn't just send a check to feed people but that we needed to help personally. I guess all of those reflect some truth and current reality, but there's another truth—one dollar feeds twenty-five to thirty-one hungry people. Perhaps we could argue about the rest after we've fed the hungry.

I Was Thirsty, and You Left Me Arid

We recall that, upon the cross, Jesus said, "I thirst" (Jn 19:28). Theologians have written countless books on Jesus's words as meaning that He thirsted for souls. We in the pews thirst for knowledge of God, of Jesus Himself, and for the experience of God's grace. I can't tell you how many times I have had to exercise great effort to keep myself from standing up in the middle of a homily to challenge the homilist on what he did or didn't say, or to plead for some satiation to my need to hear God's will for my life.

In our pews, we have homosexuals, people that suffer mental illness or who have a family member that does, young and old people that are using and abusing prescription and illegal drugs, so many who are addicted to pornography, divorced members wondering where they fit in our faith, and parents with children who are in prison. We have mothers and fathers who suffer from their decisions to abort their babies. We have all the same struggles and challenges as anyone else, and yet our church continues to be quiet in bringing Christ's words to these realities of our lives. They stop at the door of personal or individual meaningfulness. We're told to love our neighbor but not what it means to love a Democrat or a Republican, a neo-Nazi or a rapist, or even an illegal immigrant. Our politics are extreme in their divisiveness, and our church seems to be aligned with the Democratic Party, the party that promotes the so-called war on women while calling the killing of innocent babies "health care." How are we to hear God's plans for our lives when it seems one of our greatest sources for this wisdom is to come from our church, which has taken political sides against its own teaching? We're told to feed the poor, yet we never address the reality that our tax system takes so much from us that we struggle to pay our own expenses, only to see our tax revenues wasted and the number of poor increase.

We live in a culture where competition keeps us divided and working in factions against each other. We do not hear of *how* we are to be unified, just that we should be. We can't accept the illegal immigrant because they compete for our jobs and our government benefits, so how are we to engage them? We are thirsting for God's grace, but instead we receive platitudes and cute stories. It seems that the attitude from the pulpit is that we're all going to heaven, so there is no need to be controversial. Neither is there need to address sin or have expectations of holiness. I recently asked a deacon after his homily why he didn't challenge us as the prophet did in the first reading and Jesus did in the Gospel, both expecting responses from their audiences. His quick retort: "I'd get in trouble."

I Was a Stranger, and You Sent Me Away

What started me down this path of writing about the state of our church was a recent interaction I had. At our parish, we served coffee and donuts in the hall after the various Masses. One Sunday, I was sitting with our pastor and one of the head ushers. A man came in and stood nervously nearby, hesitant to engage us. Finally, he came over and spoke to the pastor about getting some help. He was out of work and just needed something to help him through the weekend until he could get to a shelter on Monday. Our pastor was rather direct with him and said that the parish office was closed and wouldn't reopen until Monday. He suggested that the man come back then. The man persisted, indicating that he had no place to sleep that night. Our pastor also persisted in his assertion that there was nothing he could do until Monday. The man began to leave, and I offered for him to help himself to some coffee and donuts, saying that I would cover the costs. As he walked away, the pastor gave a disapproving look to the usher, and the usher made a comment about the "homeless bum, probably a drunk, and we shouldn't be enabling him." I felt ashamed of our responses to this man in need. It would not surprise me if he was an alcoholic, and this was another way for him to continue in his own sin without taking responsibility for his life. But I didn't know that, and neither did our pastor or the usher. What we did know is that a man asked for help, and we turned him away. I don't think Jesus was pleased.

I Was Naked, and You Added to Your Own Comfort

A few years later, one of the deacons asked my wife to lead the Respect Life Committee. She hesitantly agreed, as my wife is not the joiner type. Although she felt uncomfortable, she has a great love for children and decided that she would trust in God for help. Not long after, she was sent a request from the diocese for a donation of $1,000 to purchase a table for the Respect Life Dinner charity event, which would raise money for the women who, having decided to keep their children rather than to abort, were in need of diapers and formula. My wife sent an email to the pastor asking for two things. First, she asked for his guidance, as she had never led a church ministry before and was in need of some counsel. Second, she requested the $1,000 for the charity table. This pastor forwarded her email to the business manager, who quite decisively advised that we had no money for the table. There was never any response from the pastor giving advice or counsel on what he expected from my spouse's leadership or management of the Respect Life ministry.

A few weeks later, I asked to see the pastor to discuss what I thought was an increased focus on the physical plant with a corresponding limiting focus on the spiritual needs of the parish. As one of my examples, I used my wife's request to support the women via the Respect Life charity event. After presenting my concern, I was told that all of the money applied to the physical plant was raised personally by the pastor and that none of the money came from the weekly collection. Although at this time I hadn't been overly concerned with the financial aspects of the question, I asked the pastor if he had likewise asked of parishioners to donate to the Respect Life table to raise money for the mothers and their infants. His response was immediate—an emphatic and dramatic change of the subject. "Bill, weren't you participating in the deaconate discernment process? How's that going?"

Collections continue to drop in our parish. On one Sunday, in lieu of a homily, we were advised that the pastor had a few projects that needed funding (a fence around the property, parking, air-conditioning) and that 30 percent of all funds raised by the various ministries would be given to the pastor to fund these initiatives. This redirection of monies from the poor and needy to the physical plant was shared after the very Gospel where Jesus tells us to "destroy this temple, and in three days I will raise it up" (Jn 2:19), reflecting on the reality that the Temple of God is not a building but is in fact the spirit of God active in the lives of the people. Yet we take money from serving the people to build up stone and mortar. A week later on Monday, I was speaking with my wife about that particular notification, and her response was, "It almost kept me from going to church yesterday."

I Was Sick, and You Visited but Too Quickly Forgot about Me

I suffered a heart attack last year and was scheduled for triple bypass surgery a few days later. I was being treated at a local Catholic hospital. I called my spiritual director, who happens to be a Catholic priest, and he came and heard my confession, gave me the sacrament of the sick, and brought me Holy Communion. In retrospect, I should have called him again, but the circumstances suggested that I didn't have to, and I also knew of his busy schedule that week. The next day was Sunday, and the assistant hospital chaplain came by, a Baptist minister who spent an hour or so with me and asked if there was anything I needed. He advised me that the hospital chaplain was off that day but would return the next. In the meantime, the associate pastor of our parish came to visit me and offered Communion. I advised him that I had already had Communion earlier that day. Frankly, I was a little surprised by the visit from the associate pastor and grateful for his prayers. He asked if there was anything I needed, and I indicated that I was to be in the hospital for a number of days and would appreciate receiving Holy Communion on a daily basis. He assured me he would take care of it. The next day, the Catholic hospital chaplain came, and as I had not received Holy Communion that day, I asked if he could arrange it. He told me that he could and would. I never saw the chaplain again, nor did I receive Holy Communion on any other day during my six-day stay.

I Was in Prison, and You Failed to Remind Your People to Come to Me

I have been a Catholic for over fifty-five years and have attended Mass for forty-five of those years. I can honestly say that I do not recall there ever being a discussion or notice in the bulletin regarding a ministry that focused on visiting those in prison. Yet after searching our local diocese's website, I found such a ministry. It seems we focus so much on ourselves that we're blinded to how the broader church engages ministries that lead to our ability to respond to God's call—in this case, to visit those in prison.

We're Called to More!

I'm sure that my reflection on this set of events does not place our pastors in a good light. I'm certainly dismayed and have expected and hoped for different outcomes. However, it would be inappropriate for me to lay all the blame of this particular situation at their feet. As Catholic parishioners, we generally donate 1.1 percent of our income to the church. Protestants average twice that, and both of us fall very short. In fact, I would estimate that in our parish we're not even meeting the national average. Is it any wonder that our pastor is led to make the decisions that he does? He is a man who realizes the importance of maintaining our facilities, of providing for the needs of the various ministries, and from his own heart has reached out to a poor parish in the Dominican Republic to offer our prayers and financial support, fulfilling Jesus' directive to care for those more in need.

What is our response, the response of the lay members of the church? The same as always, only less. We spend more money on entertainment, Starbucks coffee, expensive cars, golf, cruises, toys of all kinds, and so much more rather than return a relative portion to God by supporting our parishes. Where is our sacrifice for our neighbor? Where is our contribution to the needs of our parish and our extended church? Can we truly expect our priests and bishops to care for the needy, the poor, us—even if we don't provide them with the means? Are not the failures of our church a reflection of our own personal failures to hear and respond to what God asks?

I know these examples do not reflect well on our holy mother church, and I loathe even putting them in writing. However, they do help me remember my own sinfulness, my failures, and the inconsistencies in the expression of my faith. I cannot ignore the feeling that my failures are also our failures, and the result is that we the church have now become so cold and administrative that we no longer offer the mercy of God. It seems that we too have now become like the Pharisees. We focus on the little things, the minutiae, while neglecting weightier matters. For the Pharisees, it was a strict adherence to the washing of hands and not working on the Sabbath to the detriment of developing a clean heart and serving the poor and needy. For us, it seems we're focused on changing the words of the liturgy to be more gender inclusive and ensuring that girls may serve as altar servers, while we neglect the slaughter of innocents from our own people and for the poor and social outcasts. We demand that our church change its doctrine and rules to accommodate our changing lifestyle and cultural norms, regardless of how contrary they may be to the Word of God.

I must describe a juxtaposition of two events that I recently experienced in the same day. We moved from Tampa, Florida, to Easton, Pennsylvania, very recently, and this past weekend attended the closest Catholic church—a beautiful church, very clean, apparently new, large, seating over a thousand per Mass. This church was very bright, and the Mass was said quite efficiently. The homily, as is typical these days, was rather ordinary; the subject was the Trinity, which we were once again reminded is a mystery that cannot be explained. A few theological references, and the message was delivered. Nothing to touch the hearts of the people, nothing to challenge our lives or our faith, just nothing meaningful, frankly. Later that same afternoon, my wife and I went to her parents' house to visit. We walked into a rancid smell, a cluttered room, and her father sitting in his easy chair, mostly blind, suffering from lymphedema and legs that are about three times their normal size due to his illness. He is eighty-five years old, has been a Catholic all of his life, and still donates to his local church even though he is unable to leave the house. No one comes to visit, no confession, no Eucharist. We talk, and he cries because he's in such pain. He has to break his pain medicine into pieces because he is prescribed only a quarter of what he needs. In our talk, you can sense his frustration with the government and society but mostly the church. The religious statues and paintings covering the walls and tables of his home remind me how much religion was present in his family's life over the decades. Today, there's no church to bring him religion when he's too old and sick to matter. My heart is breaking. Where is our holy mother church?

Our religion is meant to speak to who we are as creations

of God, our dignity as given by Him, made in His likeness. Created with a need for God that will not be satisfied by any means other than finding Him. We are created in community, one body incorporated into God via the one Savior Jesus the Christ, before all of creation. And, as the philosophers tell us, from these truths there are necessary things that follow. If we have dignity from God, then each and every human has dignity that must be respected by each and every other human. If we are individuals who are joined together in community, then we can never focus exclusively on our own needs without considering the needs of others. In this truth, we find the beauty of the concept that what you do to the least ones, you've done to Jesus. This is how we love God, through loving ourselves and our neighbors. This must be so because God is one, and in Him there is no division.

Here's the rub … Our Creator asks something of His creations: turn from your sins, believe in Me, obey the Father, trust that I love you and have a plan for you and with your acceptance will grant you an eternal life of joy and happiness. In fact, he said, "I've come to set the earth on fire and wish it were already ablaze" (Lk 12:49). We don't seem too on fire at this moment, and perhaps it's because we're living as Jesus warned. While being led to his death, He spoke these words:

> Daughters of Jerusalem! Do not weep for me,
> but weep for yourselves and your children. For
> behold, the days are coming when they will say,

'Blessed are the barren, and the wombs that never bore, and the breasts that never nursed' Then they will begin to say to the mountains, "Fall on us!" and to the hills, "Cover us!" for if they do this when the wood is green, what will happen when it is dry? (Luke 23:28–30)

Am I off base when I see this reflected in today's reality? As Americans, we consume more and more psychotropic drugs, both legal and illegal. Our use of pornography and alcohol continues to climb and is at an all-time high. In a recent study, it was revealed that one in six Americans binge drinks every week. Are we not trying to hide under this mountain of medicine and diversion? Does our shame drive us to hide there rather than cry out?

To cry for God's mercy is another way of pleading for God to restore us to His will. To restore us doesn't mean to reset us to the time before the Fall—we cannot go back to the time before original sin—but it does mean to reestablish the relationship that God intends for us to have with Him. As I see it, original sin was a sin of pride above all else. We as humans have somehow accepted the idea that we could be equal to or "like" the creator. True, God made us in His image and endowed us with capabilities that are similar to His. We can create, we can choose, we can think, and we obviously have more free will than any other animal in God's creation. You can see how we might allow our egos to think that we are equal to our creator. In some deep discernment of theology, we learn that we are divinized, incorporated into God Himself, as God is one and undivided, making our temptation even more enticing. What is not true, however, is that we created God. Yet, isn't that how we live our lives—as though God doesn't exist and that we are the masters of our domain? David Platt, president of the International Missions Board of the Southern Baptist Convention, in his book *Radical* argues that this is because we accepted the lie of the American dream—with hard work and focus, we can accomplish anything, no God necessary.[2] Whereas this does explain much of our attitude in the United States, it does not explain the behavior of Catholics around the world. Original sin finds its way into our lives, regardless of our history or political or cultural beliefs and norms. We seek fulfillment, peace, serenity, and even utopia, but they never come, because we want to believe that through our seeking, creating, and living, we can somehow bring this satisfaction to our own lives. We cannot, and people throughout all of history have proved the truth of this premise. Only in God are we satisfied; only in Him do we find a lasting peace, a fulfillment of our individual and unique purpose.

I must say that as I look at myself and the world around me and encounter others who, like me, call themselves Christian, I'm dismayed. I know I'm not worthy of God's mercy. It seems that every day this world gets a little harder to bear. As an advanced modern society, we stand by as millions of unborn

---

[2] David Platt, *Radical* (2010).

children are killed in the womb. They're not just killed but cut into pieces, crushed, and gassed. Now it has come to light that some of their body parts are preserved in a way to make it easier to sell them. Anyone who speaks out against these barbaric actions is accused of waging a war on women. And many women seem to agree that the right to abortion is sacrosanct, be they Catholic, evangelical, or otherwise. Our people are divided, and, rather than try to unite us, our civil servants incite further division. Then they take our money, spend more than they take, and argue that they need still more. Yet none of our problems are solved. My employer, like so many others, operates in what can often be experienced as a hostile environment to many because of an almost constant threat of layoffs. My family has a multitude of health issues that we've spent tens of thousands of dollars and years of doctors' visits on; yet, rather than being cared for, we feel beaten down by a system that is supposed to help us. All of these add up to a lot of crosses, and the weight increases almost daily. We turn to the church with an ever-greater need, but even our church has become more of a cross than a comfort. So what are we to do now? Frankly, I'm feeling desperate, I'm crying out all the time, and I feel alone.

Yet, somehow, I still believe I'm not alone. I know in fact that this conversation is not a new one. It has been ongoing, from Moses, the apostles, the early church fathers, through Avery Dulles and into today where the discussion is being led by pastors such as Rick Warren, Joel Osteen, David Platt, Brandon

Hatmaker, and our own Pope Francis. What may be different is that the wood is much drier now, and we are closer to the time of Jesus's warning.

For those who have some measure of belief in God and either believe they should or do in fact seek His will, I will again assert that we must live as Jesus ordained. I will further propose that it is not sufficient to believe but that living according to those beliefs is crucial to our happiness and to the benefit of the world. We are not made for ourselves alone. We are members of a community. The body of Christ is one body. We each have a part to play, and the beauty of God's model is that whatever we do for another benefits ourselves. God doesn't take sides; He wants us to realize that He created us with a need for Him primarily but also within the context of needing one another. As St. James tells us, "If any one says 'I love God', and hates his brother, he is a liar" (1 Jn 4:20).

We're all called to be church—as an apostle, a disciple, healer, teacher, and comforter—and when we pass from this life to the next, Jesus said he would ask each of us the same thing, regardless of whether we're the pope, a rabbi, a minister, a layperson, an imam, or an atheist. He'll require of us to have "fed him, clothed him, given him to drink" (Mt 25:31–46). Is there any one of us who believes we're doing this to Jesus's satisfaction? If you do, you might want to stop here and put this book down. You're not likely to find anything within that will add to your good work. On the other hand, if you haven't been committing your life to God's service and have trouble even bringing yourself to Mass or to donate a few dollars to a charity, perhaps you should read on …

According to the Judeo-Christian faith, God's creation ended with the creation of man, made in the image of God. As you can surmise by now, I don't believe we quite look like the "image of God" today. Further, I think that if we did, then my cries would be heard, not just by God but by you, my brothers and sisters, and that you would respond. I'm sharing with you my opinion, my perspective, my observations as a Roman Catholic. Feel free to correct me, educate me, and lead me to a greater truth. I am open to that. In fact, I encourage it, because what I will ask of you, I'm also asking of myself. I've chosen for most of my life to act like I'm the creator of my own life, and when my creation did not respond as I planned, I blamed others or circumstances. I certainly didn't take responsibility for my choices. This was true of Eve, who blamed the serpent, Adam, who blamed Eve, and those of us who blame everything and everyone but ourselves. Having tried that approach and finding it didn't work, I now want to try believing that God is the Creator, the Author of life, and I am not. I no longer want to walk in front of God but want to follow Him. There is a residual effect of my sinfulness, and this is what I cry out against. Yes, it was my fault, my choice; still, I cry out for help. I realize that God has been reaching down to me to pull me out of the morass I created, and all I have to do is take His hand. With His pulling and my climbing, I can get free of this hell I've created. I don't have any philosophy or divinity degrees. I don't hold any position of authority in my church. In a nutshell, I suppose I'm much like you. I'm assuming, like me, you might also have a bit of a love/hate relationship with our church. What I can say to you is I'm struggling and frustrated, angry much of the time, and tired of trying to get the church to help me carry my cross. I expect that you may also be experiencing some or all of these things. Many people have told me they are, and even our Pope Francis has spoken out on behalf of all of the people of God, indicating as much for the global community.

There is hope, and I want to share with you that in my struggle I've found that my relationship with God is growing and God is active in my life. He often knocks me off my feet, not to my knees in reverence or prayer as some might expect, but to the ground. I am overwhelmed, literally by God's love, which is so much more than I can allow myself to receive. I sometimes believe I've completely surrendered what I have and who I am, but I am so limited in my ability to receive His grace that these experiences become both my heaven and hell. His love is so tender and complete, yet my inability to receive Him completely creates in me a tension that I cannot sufficiently describe. This tension pushes me to pray more fervently, to look for the sin in my life, to extinguish it, to open my heart more broadly to receive more. But there is no satisfaction because I cannot get enough. I continuously pray, "Why, Lord, will you not fill me, fill my faith, my heart, my love for you and my neighbor?" And I realize that it is me in the way, me who will not allow Him in further, who will not trust Him completely, me who still holds on to "my way."

I've come to realize that my railing against the church is in part a recognition of my need for help. I need clarity on those issues that are causing me to prevent God from entering into my life more completely. I need support for when my cross seems overwhelming. I need to feel part of a community that loves me and my family and one that, even when they can't help, can walk with me. I need the saints that are in the pews next to me to remind me that this life is temporary, that God has a bigger plan, that all things work to the benefit of those who stay grafted to the vine. I need someone to hear my cry for mercy. And, finally, I think that if I need the church to be holy and you to be holy, then you also need me to be holy. Do you want to strive to be a saint? Do you want to strive together? If we are to be saints, what should we do? What should the church do to help us in our holy endeavor?

Church Models

Perhaps we might want to step back and ask, how did our church come to such a state wherein it seems no longer relevant to the world and doesn't even serve its own? But this is a very complex question, and one beyond the scope of this book. I'd prefer to focus on where we're going rather than how we got here, except to the degree that we may need to touch on some of those issues to help us out of this morass.

Feeling the disintegration of faith in society, many are evaluating new models for the church to address the decline, and, without describing a model, many others expect Pope Francis to radically change the church or at least the rules. This is not just true of Catholics but Protestants. David Platt, in his book *Radical*, argues that we need to take back our faith from the American dream. In *Barefoot Church*, Brandon Hatmaker suggests that we should be doing a better job "serving the least in a consumer culture."[3] The importance of so many across the

---

[3] Brandon Hatmaker, *Barefoot Church* (2011).

Christian spectrum recognizing our need for transformation in no small way expresses the continuous desire of the faithful to have someone to walk with them on their journey, which can only be as a member on journey with the whole of the body of Christ.

Let's begin with a review of what Jesus found in his time, two thousand years ago. We find Jesus accusing the Jewish leaders of "loading men with burdens hard to bear and ... not touching the burdens" (Lk 11:46) to help them. We're all too familiar with their rigid focus on rules and laws to the exclusion of love of God or neighbor. Jesus reminded us then of something that is likely to be true of every age: we need constant renewal, a tearing down and a building up, until we are in fact worshipping God within our hearts. Jesus declared, "Destroy this temple and in three days I will raise it up" (Jn 2:19). To the woman at the well, He said, "The hour is coming, and now is, when the true worshipers will worship the Father in spirit and truth" (Jn 4:23).

This situation I've described always represents humankind moving away from God, and it has played out over and over again through history. Need we recall the time of the anti-popes, the Crusades, Galileo, the Inquisition, and our own most heinous of scandals, the abuse of children by priests. Our church actively covered it up and transferred these men to other places, protecting them and endangering even more children? These abuses occur when we move away from God and the

Spirit of God who leads our church and turn inward to our own selfish desires.

Our road back is not one of creating a new church but a repentance and turning away from that which takes us away from the will of God.

Avery Dulles described a set of models to explain the ways in which the church has been present to us throughout the ages. They include Mystical Communion, Sacrament, Herald, Servant, and Institution.[4] In my opinion, these are less models and might be better described as charisms of the saints of God. However, it is the institutional nature of the church that has become problematic once again. The church has become an institutionally driven organization built on a power that overshadows our communion, sacramental nature and limits our ability to herald the good news or serve our neighbor. Others can investigate and articulate the whys and hows of our current position, but suffice it to say that the church no longer serves our needs or seems sufficient to sanctify its members.

Dulles was the son of John Foster Dulles, secretary of state under President Dwight D. Eisenhower and for whom Dulles Airport in Washington, DC, is named. He was a Catholic priest and theologian. In his book *Models of the Church*, published originally in 1978, Dulles suggests that it's not possible to view the church through only one lens and expect to understand her. The premise of his approach

---

[4] Avery Dulles, *Models of the Church,* expanded edition (2005).

is that people experience certain charisms in the church and apply each to the whole as though exclusionary of all other attributes. I find this investigation into the models of the church a bit academic in its consideration; however, I think it helpful to review the overlap of the models and to consider how they integrate to provide a sense of cohesion for the historical church that most of us have experienced. I hope to build on these models as a way of considering anew how we might respond to God's call, because as you will find, I suggest that we are more church than we've allowed ourselves to consider previously. We are not just priests and laypersons but the people of God. I also think that Dulles was clearly trying to help us see how the church has been using multiple ways of presenting God to us and helping us understand the importance of not limiting it. Limiting the way we see and understand God has contributed to the divisions within the church that have generated the various sects, if you will—the Baptists, Episcopalians, Catholics, Protestants, not to mention the divisions within our own Roman Catholic sect. Let's consider each of Dulles's models so that we will have a better understanding of our church and, more importantly, the role that we should play.

Mystical Communion

This is the mystical relationship that integrates all those who live in the Spirit of God with God Himself. This communion or union of souls includes those who are still here on earth and those who have gone before us to meet God face-to-face. First Corinthians tells us, "For just as the body is one and has many members, and all the members of the body, though many, are one body, so it is with Christ. For by one Spirit we were all baptized into one body … and all were made to drink of one Spirit." In the letter of Paul to the Romans, we hear, "so we, though many, are one body in Christ, and individually members one of another." This is true regardless of location. A person having died and gone to live with God in heaven still remains a member of the one body of Christ. This mystery shrouds our ability to recognize all who are members even here on earth. Jesus tells us that "as you did it to one of the least of these my brethren, you did it to me" (Mt 25:40), and yet how often do we find ourselves confused by our failure to identify His "least ones"?

Sacrament

We learned early in life that a sacrament is an outward sign of an invisible grace. If we understand the church to be the community of the saints of the followers of Christ, we should find in our interactions with them a tangible experience of God's grace. Jesus said that "all men will know that you are my disciples, if you have love for one another" (Jn 13:35). This demonstration of love experienced by those who come in contact with the church through her members provides to all the meaning of an outward experience of the Spirit of God present and shared through the church. This is not someone who represents God to us but who *brings* God to us. It is God acting in another that brings the sacramental nature to our church experience.

Herald

Perhaps when we hear the word "herald," we think of the trumpet blasts to precede a formal declaration. To herald is to proclaim that which is heard in such a way that demonstrates to others that the proclaimer believes in what is pronounced. And what is heralded if not the good news of Christ. God so loved the world … So the church has a commission to go out and demonstrate, declare, sing, preach, and teach the good news to all the world, even to the ends of the earth.

Servant

Who of us doesn't understand a servant? But a servant who provides a service for compensation, out of duty, or under some form of dominance or control is not what we speak of here. To serve is to bring ourselves in humility to recognize that it is God who serves, who loves, who heals, who forgives our sins. We humble ourselves and invite God to use us in His service to His people, and in so doing, we find that God is praised, and we as servant are serviced as much as she who receives God's love and caring from us. This is God extending Himself to His children, to His "least ones."

Institution

In *Models of the Church*, Dulles describes the institutional nature of the church in the following way: a "view that defines the
Church primarily in terms of its visible structures, especially
the rights and powers of its officers." He says, "It will become
clear ... that the Church of Christ could not perform its mission
without some stable organizational features. It could not unite
men of many nations into a well-knit community of conviction,
commitment, and hope, and could not minister effectively to
the needs of mankind, unless it had responsible officers and
properly approved procedures."[5] I don't agree with this description in its entirety. It is certainly true that as a group grows in
size, it requires organization, and there is certainly an element
to the visible structure enabling and enhancing the ability of
men and women to associate their work with its organization
and founder. However, this is mostly true when the members
act according to the teachings and directions of Jesus. It is when
we are united with Christ that we are effective with spreading
the good news and the love of God. Consider St. Francis of
Assisi, Mother Teresa, and others who made a great impact
on behalf of the Christian faith, even prior to support of the
institutional church, or even while at odds with her. I think
now of the good works done by those Protestant and schismatic
churches who still bring the good news.

---

[5] Avery Dulles, *Models of the Church*, expanded edition (2005), 27.

A New Framework—
We Feed Them!

Although Dulles does a wonderful job of explaining the ways in which the church was perceived in days past, today most people don't consider the church at all, except to think of it as being opposed to abortion and gay marriage or to consider scandals. I believe the reason for this is because the church has become mostly irrelevant to the current American and European cultures.

But what if we considered Dulles's models from a different perspective? They could be readily presented as models of essence, of action, and of organization. Mystical Communion speaks to our status or existence as a member of the body of Christ. We do not determine it; it preexists us and is in reality the existence of Christ Himself. We are invited to join through baptism, a gift of God Himself to offer us a place within His very own existence. Humans become divine. However, we are also reminded that we must remain in Him. When we remain living in Him, we become sacrament—the visible sign of God's presence. As members, we act as Christ directed, "Go therefore and make disciples of all nations, baptizing them in the name of the Father and of the Son and of the Holy Spirit, teaching them to observe all that I've commanded" (Mt 28:19). These are to be the actions of the church: herald the good news and be servant of all. The last model, institution, is the natural result of the expansion of this spreading of the kingdom of God. We must maintain our presence in Christ and our service to one another. Expansion happens through a scaling of the growth of the kingdom within those who believe. Growth demands a higher level of organization, which is what the institution of the church is intended to represent. This organization becomes deformed when it takes power on itself and attempts to create itself in its own image. Let us recall from Paul's letter to the Philippians that Jesus, "who, though he was in the form of God, did not count equality with God a thing to be grasped, but emptied himself, taking the form of a servant" (Philippians 2:6–7).

I propose that the church needs to revert back to its original state. However, before we look back to evaluate what we should reinstitute in our lives and practices, we might consider that which each saint has and must understand as the driving force of their behavior. Let us look ahead to our end, to the moment we stand before Christ for judgment. In response to a question regarding our entry into heaven, Jesus described the following:

Then the king will say to those at his right hand, 'Come, O blessed of my Father, inherit the kingdom prepared for you from the foundation of the world; for I was hungry and you gave me food; I was thirsty and you gave me drink; I was a stranger and you welcomed me; I was naked and you clothed me; I was sick and you visited me; I was in prison and you came to me.' Then the righteous will answer him, 'Lord, when did we see you hungry, and feed you; or thirsty, and give you drink? And when did we see you a stranger, and welcome you; or naked, and clothe you? And when did we see you sick or in prison, and visit you?' And the king will answer them, 'Truly I say to you, as you did it to one of the least of these my brethren, you did it to me.' (Matthew 25:34–40)

Jesus also said, "You call me Teacher and Lord; and you are right, for so I am. If I then, your Lord and Teacher, have washed your feet, you also ought to wash one another's feet. For I have given you an example, that you also should do as I have done to you" (Mt 20:25).

At the end of time when judgment will occur or upon the death of each of us individually, we will stand before God and be judged. And so our Judge aids us in understanding the law. In an absolutely effective and beautiful way, we learn that the law is fulfilled in our love of God and service to one another.

This is the measure by which all of us and each of us will be judged. Therefore, the church being the institution of God—or the organizing principle, if you will—is missioned with bringing us to Christ to answer these in the affirmative.

We could speak to the many ways and reasons in which we go astray of this judgment. We could blame our human needs, our media, the divided world in which we find ourselves. However true these things are, we can work to change all of them. It is incumbent upon us to recognize that in its simplicity today, we can in fact follow Christ's command: spread the good news, love your neighbor, feed me …

But how?

Let's look to the saints, whom we know to be good models of how we are to live. Let's even go so far as to listen and respond to Jesus's directives. Let's not ask, "What would Jesus do?" in any situation, but rather, "What did He say that we should do?"

In the scriptures, we find John the Baptist making way the path of the Lord. He preaches a ministry of repentance, a turning from the ways of this world to the ways of God. Jesus comes, and the first command that we find him utter as recorded in the scriptures is, "Repent." At the founding of the church, we find the apostles, having received the Holy Spirit, begin preaching repentance. St. Paul and Barnabas, when confronted by the people of Lystra and Iconium as gods themselves, plead with them to not consider them as gods but to hear the good news and respond with a heart of repentance.

It's still true and, in fact, is possibly truer now than ever— we must turn from the world. Jesus doesn't just leave us with a command to turn from what destroys us but provides us the alternative that saves us. "I am the Way, and the Truth, and the Life" (Jn 14:6). The only name under heaven that brings salvation is the name of Jesus. Except through Him no one can enter into the kingdom of heaven. Believe!

Religious phrases and ideologies such as these may not resonate with many who haven't heard the Gospel or the teachings of Christ today. In the days of old, Jesus came to a world filled with religion, the Jews with their one God and the Romans and Greeks with their many. Today, neither God nor gods are so much in favor, but we can look to the reality of our experiences to see the truth of the destruction, division, and detriment of this world. We can look to our own lives and know that we're isolated, confused, and struggling. Our use of drugs, alcohol, sex, and materialism doesn't keep us from the constant reminders of the realities of our lives. We are indeed turning and constantly turning, but to what? The issue isn't that we need to be reminded that we should turn; it's, to what should we turn? What we've been turning to is not only not working but adding to our misery.

We need the good news. Who will bring it? The saints!

Jesus came and spent three years developing men and women to be saints. He then returned to the Father so that He could send them the Holy Spirit, upon receipt of whom they changed from fearful men hidden in an upper room to men of courage, conviction, and power who went out and preached the good news until death—eleven of the twelve dying as martyrs. Where do we find the saints today?

It is said that the devil once told St. John Vianney, "If there were three such priests as you, my kingdom would be ruined."[6] This was true, not just because Vianney was a priest but because he was a saintly priest.

We understand from our review of *Models of the Church* that the church is present to us in the sacramental nature of those who live in communion with God. We call those people saints. In the development of the early church, we saw the saints go out into the world to preach and serve. They healed, fed, drove out evil spirits, and walked with the people. They stayed with the people to help them understand what it meant to live in the Spirit and for the kingdom of God. I once had a spiritual director ask me what I was seeking, and I responded that I wanted to be a saint. He put his hand on my head and said, "Be a saint!" In the simplest way, he helped me to understand that I could be a saint, but to attain that goal, I had to "be" what I desired. I believe that we are each called to be saints, some as religious, priests, nuns; others as lay persons. The most important thing to remember is that you and I are not called to be Mother Teresa or St. Francis of Assisi. Neither are we called to be Pope Francis

---

[6] Abbe Francis Trochu, *The Cure D'Ars: St. Jean-Marie Baptiste Vianney.*

or Mother Cabrini; what we are called to be is Saint you and Saint me. Saints, not because we would do what other saints have done but saints because we sought God, listened to His call, and responded as only we can. In that response, we can rightly be called followers of Christ. How do we advance in the ways of God?

To the Layperson at Home and in the Pews

To experience the reality of this loving, merciful God, we need an encounter with Jesus the Christ, the Son within the Trinity. This experience comes for most of us through the experience of meeting a saint, and the absence is equally felt. Gandhi is quoted as reflecting on this absence: "I like your Christ, I do not like your Christians. Your Christians are so unlike your Christ." Our Christ spoke mainly about very simple things, things we all know and experience—a hunger for something greater than this, something deeper, something worth dying for. We find this simplicity in the lives of those who believe in Jesus Christ and are living as sacrament in the world. And of what will they remind us?

Again, they will remind us first to repent, to turn from this world and its trappings and pursuits that lead us away from God. They show us how to turn to God and believe. Be baptized, keep the sacraments, and pray so that you may remain in Him. Humble yourself and exalt God. Sing His praises, worship Him. Trust everything to God. Then serve your neighbor, and, in doing so, you will serve Christ Himself. You'll have a cross to bear, and you must pick it up every day and carry it. Remember to seek first the kingdom of God, and then all else will be added unto you. "Let your light so shine before men, that they may see your good works and give glory to your Father who is in heaven" (Mt 5:16).

If you're over fifty, you've probably heard these things many times before. If under fifty, perhaps you've never heard them. Regardless, what does all this mean?

If you decide to repent, to turn away from living according to the world and turn to God, you then must commit an act of your will—to believe. Believing, you will want to communicate with your God, to speak with Him and open your heart to hear Him speaking to you. You will humble yourself, because in the presence of God, we cannot help ourselves. (At this point, you may be turned off by my use of the masculine. Please understand that I realize that God is spirit and therefore not male nor female; however, Jesus referred to God as the Father, so I follow His lead. Please feel free to think of God as either or neither, whichever helps you.) To humble ourselves before God means to realize that we are not God the Creator but His creation. You are His, and you were created to know, love, and yes, even to serve Him. You will not want to serve Him if you don't love Him, and you will not love Him if you don't know Him. You'll need to spend time getting to know Him. That means time dedicated to your relationship with God, time in prayer, and time reading and studying sources that help you become familiar with the things of God. Your study and your investigation will most assuredly help you know about God, and more importantly, your prayer will deepen your relationship with Him.

Practically, the results of this effort will include giving up those things that separate you from God and your neighbor. These may include drugs, alcohol, pornography, gambling, and the constant seeking of fun and entertainment. It would mean that "what happens in Vegas" is confessed rather than kept secret. Further, it means putting others' needs ahead of your own. Rather than demanding more rights for yourself, you will find yourself working to ensure that the basic human rights of others are promoted and effectual. In politics, it means that you will stop seeing your neighbor as an enemy because they support the other candidate and will start working with that neighbor to solve the problems of your community. It means that you'll stop spending so much of your money on cigarettes, wine, and psychotropic medications or your time on pornography, sports, and entertainment to escape from the reality that you have a cross to bear. It means that you'll pick up your cross, thank God for it, and ask in prayer to unite your suffering with His. It doesn't mean that you won't have any more fun or entertainment, won't enjoy music, art, sex, or a drink, but it does mean that you'll learn to seek the kingdom first. It means to put all of these things to the service of God.

God wants your happiness, your complete joy, your salvation, and finally wants you to be with Him through all of eternity. He has given you all things that you may know Him and that your joy might be complete. Return to Him a portion of what He has given to you. You do this to demonstrate your gratitude, which will grow as you come to understand what grace and mercy He has afforded you. In your gratitude, you will realize ever more deeply that He is taking care of everything for you. He has fed you, clothed you, provided your care. If you can't see that in your life, look at Mother Teresa of Calcutta. She left her order and went to serve the poorest of the poor. Keep in mind, she left with nothing. She was in fact as poor as those she was to serve, and yet her love and sacrifice were sufficient to enable the service of thousands and tens of thousands.

Finally, seek out a community, a church to share in the worship service and the love of God and to have access to the support that will come from your community for yourself. Carrying your cross will be challenging at times; you'll need help carrying it or comfort as you carry it yourself. You'll also find that others in your community can help you come closer to God, to share in prayer, in reflection and in discerning God's voice. Remember that part of your effort must be to financially support your church. God asks us to tithe, to give 10 percent off the top. Do so willingly in response to the great and generous gifts that God has already bestowed on you and because only by being responsive to what He asks of you can you be sure that you are walking in faith. In a nutshell, desire to live a saintly life.

For Our Institutional Church Leaders

Herald the good news and be servant of all. Preach and teach us to serve God. Recall when Jesus called the twelve apostles together and said:

> You know that the rulers of the Gentiles lord it over them, and their great men exercise authority over them. It shall not be so among you; but whoever would be great among you must be your servant, and whoever would be first among you must be your slave even as the Son of man came not to be served but to serve. (Mt 20:25–28)

It is clear that the church, although having once been both the religious authority and so intertwined in government authority that there was no difference, presents no risk today of lording over the people. I would argue that they don't even exercise religious authority any longer, to the clear detriment of the faith. The move to a more secularized institution has stripped the church of even its moral authority. The answer is not to return to power but to return to providing the service Jesus demanded with the authority of God, who multiplies our work for the benefit of His creation.

So get off the altar. Yes, the Eucharist is the source and summit of our faith, but there is also something in between.

From the source, you are called to go out and bring the good news to the people and then to bring the people to the summit of our faith, Christ in the blessed sacrament. God is the beginning and the end, but you must do your part, which is in the in between. Do you not realize how inwardly focused you are? Dulles speaks to the need for the contrary, "This ecclesiological model calls for a conception of priesthood that does not turn inward on the Church itself, but outward to the larger society of mankind."[7] We barely reach the people in our pews, let alone reach outward to our larger community in any practical way. We've organized our service around specific disciplines—the Saint Vincent De Paul Society or Catholic Charities to serve the poor, Catholic hospitals to serve the sick, Catholic universities to serve the educational needs of our children. This separateness—even division—is contradictory to the teaching of Christ to be of one mind and as one body, leveraging the many gifts to the service of one God. And who serves the needs of the people in the pews, called to be sent out, to carry their cross, to serve their neighbor? Who serves our need to be more united? Why do we continue to fail God's people? And what of our programs? Do they even work? For Jesus, to be at work meant taking two loaves and five fish, asking God to bless them, and then feeding five thousand men, not to mention the women and children. I recently heard from our parish St. Vincent de Paul leader that after eight years of existence, our parish of four thousand families is feeding two hundred on a monthly basis,

---

[7] Dulles, *Models of the Church*, expanded edition (2005), 164.

and we applauded this effort as successful. Clearly, those who donate their time, money, talents, and love have participated in God's charity, but what of the rest of us?

You too focus on the kingdom! Neither should the clergy be concerned with what they need to conduct their ministry. Stop relying on programs and requests and secular ways of raising money. Return to trusting that God provides for you and that the key to opening the coffers of God is not based on your fundraising skills but on your faith, trust, and gratitude.

"Therefore do not be anxious, saying, 'What shall we eat?' or 'What shall we drink?' or 'What shall we wear?' For the Gentiles seek all these things, and your heavenly father knows that you need them all. But seek first his kingdom and his righteousness, and all these things shall be yours as well" (Mt 6:32–33).

You know what Christ will ask each of us at our death. This is the same for everyone. Enable our church to redesign our composition, organization, mission, and focus such that we will empower our members to meet this expectation and ask of Christ, "Lord, when did we see you hungry and feed you or thirsty and give you drink?" (Mt 25:37). This must be the measure of success. Lead us to a change in our own realization of our place along faith's journey. Expect our people to grow in faith. Stop maintaining our slow decline and start expecting and requiring the growth of the kingdom of the people of God. If we were a business with a mission of saving souls, we'd be out of business. Sales are way down! Certainly you can say that God never goes out of business and souls are being won for Christ, but can we honestly say that it's because we're doing our part? We needn't look far to see how we might simplify our structure to be more effective. Our recently canonized Mother Teresa shows us an organizational structure that seems to be a good example of how this might be pursued. She had minimal hierarchy, only the facilities needed to serve the poor, and an attitude to walk among them. Of this, God blessed her and worked His will. Why do you live in mansions with servants (called volunteers), cooks, cleaning personnel, and administrators? If you're a pastor or a bishop, you even have gatekeepers and designated officials to buffer you from engaging the needs of the people you're called to serve. Mother Teresa, a saint and a wonderful example of service to all, may not have had the responsibilities of the priesthood or administration of the church, but because she placed her will and service at the direction of God, she has accomplished more in the service of the church than have most priests and pastors.

A Merciful Church Is
a Saintly Church!

S o what is this new model of church I'm suggesting? In fact, it's not new at all. What I'm proposing is a resurrection of the original church—the church of saints. What did Jesus do and say we should do? What did the apostles, who were given the keys of the kingdom, do and say we should do? How did they operate? St. Paul reminds us of the validity of this approach in 1 Corinthians, "Imitate me as I imitate Christ." You are called to lead the way!

"In the institutionalist ecclesiology the powers and functions of the Church are generally divided into three: teaching, sanctifying, and governing."[8] I'm not overly comfortable with the governing part, but what I do believe is that a person educated in the ways of our Lord and sanctified must require little governance, as they would naturally want to live in the freedom

---

[8] Avery Dulles, *Models of the Church*, expanded edition (2005), 29, 30.

granted the children of God. Why not begin with a focus on making saints of the people in the pew who will respond in the affirmative to the final judgment of Christ?

The Catholic Church says it has 1.1 billion members, which is at best an exaggeration, as we're likely the only organization in the world where its members can deny every organizing principal and its principles, declaim their membership, and yet still be counted among the membership. Regardless of this, it is still likely true that we are potentially the largest organized set of resources on the planet. Why don't we have a greater impact? Because the church has become more about ourselves, our power, our ego, and our purpose than contributing in service to God's will. Every action, every direction, must be executed in the context of "seeking first the Kingdom of God" (Mt 6:33). There can be no deviation from this directive; when we follow it, "all else is given to us" (Mt 6:33) to enable us to serve God's will and make real what we ask. "Thy will be done on earth as it is in heaven" (Mt 6:10). From an institutional perspective, we heard early on from Peter that the church leaders cannot do everything required of the people they serve. The role of the church leaders is to pray and teach the Word of God. It's also clear that they were to exercise their priestly ministry with the laying on of hands. Scholars and others have presented that the church as an institution is called to teach, sanctify, and govern. In many, if not most, of our parishes, our priests have delegated the distribution of food to others—St. Vincent de Paul Society or Catholic Charities. But rather than using their time to preach and teach, they use the time to govern. Let's start there.

Govern

We are taught of the primacy of Peter; however, I think we promote Peter's primacy from the wrong angle. Jesus did not tell the other apostles, "Listen to Peter. I put Peter above you." No, he told Peter, "Feed my sheep, tend my sheep" (Jn 21:16–17). Let's remember that Jesus had just demonstrated the kind of service he intended as he washed the feet of the apostles. And St. Paul also reminds us the nature of service when he told husbands to love their wives as Christ loves the church. What authority does Peter need to do this? Jesus said, "Who made me a judge or divider over you?" (Lk 12:14). "Do not lord over … but serve" (Mt 20:25–26). The church was built to serve, yet I cannot even speak to my bishop without his gatekeeper blocking my call. How can he serve me if he doesn't know me?

An organization must have clear leadership and direction. There also needs to be an element of learning and a flexible framework for certain activities to be executed relative to local requirements. Jesus Christ is the leader of our church. He gave a clear set of guidelines and allows the organizational requirements I suggest above. I'll highlight them in a bit, but let us again recall that the church is one body, Christ as head, with Christians joined together—clergy and laypersons—as the body, including those here on earth and those already present to the face of God. Together we bring the presence of God to the world. St. Paul tells us that the body is one, with many parts. Later we heard that the Spirit provides different gifts. Let us understand these in the context of the needs of the church: feeding the poor, visiting the sick, consoling, clothing the naked, giving drink, teaching, preaching, and governing.

Let's begin with asking, "Why aren't our ministries jointly developed?" We know that groups and ministries that come together and work as a community with a common mission serve more effectively. We should also change our approach to funding our needs. Stop asking for money for every potential event; one day it's the air conditioner, next the roof, the new pavilion, the statue. Let's develop a tithing parish. God said give back to Him a tenth off the top, the first fruits, and if you do, He will bless you in abundance. Why do we not seek abundance for our people?

Consider a simple example to illustrate how far off we are from serving our community. I've got to believe that in our parish on a Sunday, there is a man, let's say a plumber, who prays for an opportunity to serve his neighbor. This man may one day stand next to an elderly woman who prays for God's assistance with a situation she has at home. It seems she has a leaky faucet. She lives on a fixed income and cannot afford the $200 to hire a plumber to fix the faucet. Let's further say that the leak is costing this woman thirty dollars a month in wasted water bills. Would it be hard to imagine that it would be easy for our church to connect these two members of the parish? Yet it rarely happens. Imagine what a difference to the lives of these two and the broader parish at large. With his assistance, she might avoid the costs associated with the leak. In turn, she might donate a portion of her savings to the church, enabling the church to help those whom they turn away due to a lack of funds. This may seem so simple, but it doesn't happen. This woman, assuming she reached out, is more likely to be referred from her local church to Catholic Charities. She almost certainly would not be connected with the man we described. This would be too risky in our secular institutionalism, where our concern is more with the legal risk and potential liability if something were to go wrong.

The church must provide means and support for our mission to feed the poor, clothe the naked, and educate and comfort our neighbors. We have many good examples. We can think of Mother Teresa and St. Francis of Assisi to remind us of the difference between a secular-driven service versus a saint acting in the service of God.

Get rid of everything else. Evaluate what structures, disciplines, or organizational constructs are necessary for the church to be the holy community of Catholic saints.

Because each of us will be asked if we've lived the beatitudes, it follows that the church must enable its members to do so. God has gifted the members of our community with the many skills necessary to build organizations, education systems, and distribution networks in order to serve our call to love others. We must remember to carry out this work within the context of God's will and plan, and with His grace, but we must also remember to think and act as God's cocreators in the work of the kingdom and do our part.

We must have an absolutely limited hierarchy in the governance of the church. Jesus said, "I call you friends" (Jn 15:15). As brothers, we have one king, Christ. Let us serve together. Power is always a limiting dynamic, amassing to a smaller and smaller number of people, but service is an expansive dynamic and can include all of us. Even the poorest of the poor can participate because they provide to the rest of us the opportunity to serve Christ—and what greater exercise of service is there than bringing us to the Creator? When the church returns to treating parishioners as members of the same community, each acting under and through the Holy Spirit of God, each with the same mission to teach and to sanctify, then isn't it reasonable to believe that they would at times provide these services to those who lead the institutional church? Let's not think of this as a sharing of power but of service, which we know enables a stronger community.

To move from the secular pull of power to a position of servant suggests that the Catholic Church consider giving up its tax-exempt status. This would have a dramatic impact on the church's financial position, at least initially. It is estimated that there are over seventeen thousand parishes in the United States, and each has property associated with it; the real estate taxes avoided total in the billions per year. Donations to these parishes also total billions per year and are exempt of federal income tax. However, along with these financial benefits, there are government regulations that affect the church's ability to speak out on certain issues and also prevents the church from engaging in political recommendations to its members. Although the amounts are significant, assuredly we can rely on God to make up what is needed to serve his people. But most importantly is the effect of limiting the church's role in speaking to the heart of the people, especially in the public discourse, which must by definition include involving itself, even if on the periphery of politics. We also must stop aligning with politicians and realize that, in reality, politics does not operate according to the good that it can do for the many but according to the power it can provide the few. The church sees a great value and service in politics, providing an opportunity to men and women of good will to serve. However, politics does not fulfill its purpose and today is almost exclusively about promoting the division of the people and taking advantage of their needs in order to amass and keep power for a very small group, including those in public office, wealthy individuals, and powerful business leaders. A critical study of Jesus's engagement with governmental authority helps us understand its authority as granted by God, but our involvement must be limited in our roles as citizens. Recall that His strongest teaching on this subject was to remind us not to be of this world, however involved we must be in it. It seems of late that our church has lost its way on this matter, especially here in the United States. We've gone so far as to be clearly perceived as aligning with the Democratic Party in the United States, which now is mandating that we pay for abortion and is actively working to remove the religious freedom of our people. It would not be too radical to state that we have literally gotten into bed with the devil. Our current politic is rightfully described as diabolic.

We needn't look to politics to see the aberration of the use of power. In the institutional church, there is an intrinsic evil in the way that many parishes are run. The pastor appoints the council that monitors him. He also appoints the finance committee members who are supposed to represent a balance, but as his appointees work to serve him rather than the community they are missioned to serve, they instead only serve the further amassing of power. This is a dominance and control that is not serving the people of God. Let's have the priests refocus their authority. God Himself created us and immediately invited us to name the animals. By doing so, He showed us early on His intention to engage His people as cocreators. Yet few pastors administer their parishes with an equal trust and engagement of their parishioners, who will almost always add to the resources available to the pastor, whether they be administrative, leadership, organization, marketing, or communications. All of these skills are available to improve the operation of our local communities.

I think, for example, about a core group of people from the RCIA and the faith formation groups who sit together, pray together, and discuss together how we might have an impact on the people that come to our parish for faith formation or for the sacraments. These same people then serve their community as Eucharistic ministers, catechists, and mentors. They are also the ones found donating to the poor, serving the needs of the parish, and as role models at their work locations and in their neighborhoods. Perhaps an expansion of this behavior could extend to a group led by the pastor with the parish clergy, other leaders from the various groups, including the council, financial, stewardship, liturgical committees, and all ministries to come together as one mind and one community. We would put our issues before God, asking Him to bless us. Only then would we begin to discuss and evaluate solutions to the challenges that face us. Our primary effort would begin with getting to know the people in our own pews. Who are they? What do they do? What challenges to they have in their lives? What crosses do they bear? What do they ask of the church? How can the church be of assistance to them? How might the church facilitate their meeting and supporting others walking this pilgrimage, especially those sitting next to them in the pews? Once determined, we would then act on behalf of service of God and neighbor. This is the governance Jesus directed, "Strengthen your brothers" (Lk 22:32), and as Paul reminded, "I complete what is lacking in Christ's afflictions for the sake of His body, that is the Church" (Colossians 1.24). In this way, our church is at the service of its members, who in turn reach out.

Preach

The twelve said, "It is not right that we should give up preaching the word of God to serve tables … but we will devote ourselves to prayer and to the ministry of the word" (Acts 6:2). This ministry of the Word includes preaching, teaching, and exercising the sacraments.

Preach the good news. This is not telling stories but helping people enter into the Word of God, helping them to come to speak with God through hearing His Word. Preaching must challenge us as Jesus did, with specific directions, rather than rules set and left to themselves, in order to engage people in the process of "working out salvation in fear and trembling" (Philippians 2:12). Preaching needs to be one of talking to the people in their lives where they are and then sharing and using God's Word to talk to those issues. Bring God into their lives so they have the courage and wisdom to deal with those issues that are the same today as they've always been. St. Francis of Assisi reminded us that preaching should only be done by words when necessary, that true preaching was modeling and living in persona Christi. In other words, preach by example.

John the Baptist was not known for telling stories or parables but for providing clear instruction. "Rob no one by violence or by false accusation, and be content with your wages" (Lk 3:14). After the parable of the Good Samaritan, Jesus told the lawyer, "Go and do likewise" (Lk 10:37). When the

Pharisees brought the woman caught in adultery to Jesus, He sent her away with a directive, "Go and do not sin again" (Jn 8:11). This is the power that Jesus wants you to exercise—to forgive sins and to heal the people. But how can you do this when you ignore the realities of the people in the pews? When your homilies stop after the story and fail to engage us at the personal level, you fail to preach the good news. We mustn't ever forget that we're sinners who have need of repentance. When you preach as though you are writing short stories for literary purposes rather than speaking with the authority of God to the needs of the people, you do us the greatest disservice. Stop treating us as though we all come to church because we're good and holy people. You know otherwise. We don't demonstrate gratitude to God by giving a portion back to Him, yet you pat us on the head when we put pennies in the collection. We are comparable in our support of abortion, and more than the secular public are in favor of same-sex marriage, yet you rarely mention them.

Deliver the sacraments to people who seek to grow in the spirit, no longer as a ritual norm but to deliver the efficacy and power of which it contains, Christ. To do so, you yourselves must be spending your own time in the presence of the Eucharist and in a deep and abiding prayer relationship. From an abiding trust in Jesus, expect the people in the pews to be holy and to become saints, which may require you to walk with them for a time, even a lifetime.

Teach

In Acts 14, we hear, "So they remained for a long time, speaking boldly for the lord, who bore witness to the word of his grace, granting signs and wonders to be done by their hands … and they remained no little time with the disciples."

Teach us to pray! Teach us how to live in the world rather than of it. Make an example of the institutional church. Extricate yourselves from government entanglement. We know that power corrupts, and service is the only antidote. Model service such that the people would know what to expect from their government. If you learn from government, how many more evils will you cover up to protect your own power?

Teaching presents a clear direction for the work of our priests and bishops. Pastors and priests must spend "no little time with the people," who need to come to understand God. In the homily of his first Chrism Mass after being elected in 2013, Pope Francis urged priests to "go out" and to live with the "odor of the sheep." This is so necessary, especially for our times, and yet our leaders are still locked away in their protective rooms, hidden behind their busy schedules.

Help the lay person to be sacramental by teaching them to grow in faith and service. Teach them the way to herald the good news. Help them understand God's forgiveness and mercy, not just in the confessional but through your engagement. Walk with them as brothers and sisters on their road to

Emmaus. Do this by enabling parishioners to love their neighbor through service.

Even in our institutions of learning, our schools and universities, we should teach, first to love God, to practice prayer and union with God. Then with the grace of God, teach academics but always according to the truth that Christ taught and imitated and not as the world teaches. Too often, our schools and universities are best at teaching us how to be "of the world." We are very successful at teaching to be successful as the world measures, and in doing so, we teach our children to put the world first, to seek what is temporal versus what is eternal. In the end, this focus only further develops our people to be used in the consumer-driven machine serving mammon. Teach people to realize the reality of their lives, having been created by and for God. Teach us to be saints.

Jesus focused on developing apostles and disciples. Nothing we do will change what Jesus said about the end-times. He asked, "When the Son of man comes, will he find faith on earth?" (Lk 18:8). He responded to his disciples' question about when the end of the age would be with a warning: "Then they will deliver you up to tribulation, and put you to death; and you will be hated by all nations for my name's sake. And then many will fall away, and betray one another, and hate one another. And many false prophets will arise and lead many astray. And because wickedness is multiplied, most men's love will grow cold" (Mt 24:9-12). Jesus also adds, "But he who endures to the end will be saved. And this gospel of the kingdom will be preached throughout the whole world, as a testimony to all nations; and then the end will come" (Mt 24:9, 13–14). Teach us to be prepared.

We study doctrine and theology in our seminaries, but what of holiness, saintliness? If we judge by what we find in our priests, it seems that the monasteries and cloisters are for holiness, which is kept locked away, but seminaries are for worldliness.

Our patron saint of missionaries, St. Teresa of Lisieux, never left her cloister, yet she was able to reveal to us how God's will is served. He turned her openness to His will and her willingness to place her sacrifice at His service to the blessing of others.

People say they don't have enough money to give the church, and yet they have plenty for entertainment and responding to the demands of our consumerist culture. Why don't our priests teach us gratitude? God provides for all we have, so why not trust him to provide all that we need? Let's stop focusing on the nickels and dimes and start focusing on the love that God wants to share with us. He will provide for our needs. He tells us to not be worried about the food and drink we need to stay alive or about our bodies. Our Father in heaven knows that we need all these things. Instead, He advises us to be concerned about the kingdom of God and what He requires of us, and He will provide us with all these other things. Let's help the people focus on those things that God requires of them to pray, love, and serve, and let God take care of the money. Let's give it back to him and let Him multiply it and feed the five and ten thousand. Let's trust because He's trustworthy. This change in attitude and expectations would start to address the material needs of our church but would also address the spiritual energy and dynamic that we need from the people. Jesus turned to his apostles and said, "You give them something to eat" (Mt 14:16). He told Peter, "Feed my lambs, tend my sheep!" (Jn 21:15–16). Let's tear down the buildings and bring the people together to build a living church, a living monument to God that is the loving care for the people around us.

Service Is for All of Us!

St. Paul wrote his letters to the Christians of the various cities where he founded churches or spent significant time converting the gentiles. His teachings are good for reflection by we who are the lay apostolate, because of their richness and for their direction on how we should live out our faith. Paul reminds us that we are called for service and describes for us the many and varied ways in which we can serve. We are not all called to serve in the same way, but we are all called to serve:

> And his gifts were that some should be apostles, some prophets, some evangelists, some pastors and teachers, to equip the saints for the work of ministry, for building up the body of Christ, until we all attain to the unity of the faith and

of the knowledge of the Son of God. (Ephesians
4:11–16)

We recognize that the church has been granted certain
powers by God; however, we must be careful not to allow those
powers to become a divisive teaching as the world would use
between the lord and servant. The division of the teacher and
the taught suggests that one has more than the other. Might
it not be truer to see each as needing from the other and each
as providing to the other? In this view, there is an inherent
equality as children of God. Otherwise, we have issues that
challenge our humility. If one is exclusively the teacher, then the
student is subservient. All of us are both students and servants
of God. We call Him Lord and Savior; He is Jesus the Christ.
When we move to governing, we then have one person lording
over another. Jesus made it clear that we are not to be like the
heathens who act accordingly. Let it be that the teacher serves
the student, the sanctifier serves those in need of sanctification,
and the governor serves the needs of the governed. And let the
student, those in need of sanctification, and the governed be a
reminder and a teacher of the humility of God. How far we are
from this when the governor is too busy administering to be
present to those in need.

For our priests: serve by delivering the sacraments, by walking and leading, and by modeling the actions of a saint. Recall
that in the early church, having realized the need to refocus
the work of the apostles, they decided to select "seven men of

good repute, full of the Spirit and of wisdom." They "devoted themselves to prayer and the ministry of the word ... and the word of God increased" (Acts 6:4–7). Strengthen your brothers; provide communities, support structures, and opportunities to worship and pray together, to uplift our neighbor when they fall, and to stay the course.

Consider the following example:

Your brother saint, St. Thomas of Villanova:

In 1565, Thomas, an Augustinian canon, preacher, and scholar, was appointed archbishop of Valencia, Spain. A bishop had not been in residence there for a century, and disorder reigned among the people and the clergy. Thomas started with the people. He went from town to town to meet them. He saw where they lived, looked at them with eyes of mercy, and then preached to them of hope for eternal salvation.

Thomas started many "programs." His bishop's palace became a veritable soup kitchen for upwards of 500 people a day, where he served food and wine. He provided dowries for women who wanted to marry but could not. He gave tools to tradesmen who had fallen on hard times. Foundlings were his favorites; Thomas paid a

finder's fee to anyone who brought him an abandoned child.

Some complained that the poor took advantage
of Thomas. He answered that it was not his job
to find the cheats among them—that was for
the authorities. His job was to give when asked.
In his life they called him "the almsgiver," "the
father of the poor," and "the model of bishops."
Not a few miracles of multiplication were at-
tributed to him. His energy came from prayer,
fervent and frequent, the habit of his youth.[9]"

Thomas was an archbishop, yet even in his high position,
it was he who fed the people, provided dowries for the women,
gave tools to the tradesmen. He was pro-women and prolife.
He became known for his charitable works, but perhaps more
importantly, we find that his successes were the result of "fervent and frequent prayer," praying for the eternal salvation of
his people, whom he went out to meet "where they lived" and
"with eyes of mercy."

For the rest of us: Mother Teresa showed us clearly how
to serve, and I needn't describe the well-known works of this
modern saint. Let's follow them.

---

[9] Lisa Lickona, *Magnificat Year of Mercy Companion* (New York: Magnificat, Inc., 2015), 363.

May the Fire Burn!

I hear Jesus's words, "I've come to set the world on fire and wish that it was already ablaze" (Lk 12:49), which I believe are calling us to do our part. In the description of the miracle of the loaves, when the apostles asked Jesus to send the people away so that they could get something to eat, He turned to them and said, "You feed them!" (Mt 14:16). When the disciples returned from having been sent out and advised Jesus that they cast out demons and healed people in His name and were excited to have had the experience of exercising these powers, Jesus reminded them that these powers are not to be valued so much as having our names written in the book of life. These reminders weigh heavily on my mind and heart. True service requires us to be a member of the one mystical community and to remain in Christ throughout our lives as a sacrament reflecting God to those who experience us. It further requires us to share the good news and to serve our neighbor. Of course, as we continue to be successful in this world, we will want to benefit from the abilities of a growing community, which requires the use of institutional constructs. We've seen how corrosive institutionalism can be when we turn from using an organizational mechanism to support the will of the Holy Spirit to our own selfish human desires. Let us once again dedicate ourselves to stripping down these artificially created divisions and practices and focus our time and energies on hearing the cries of the people. Perhaps you will hear even mine, and I may find support in my own personal journey back to God.

Sources

1. Amos 8:11–12, Ignatius Bible, revised standard edition, 2nd Catholic edition (San Francisco: Ignatius Press, 2005).
2. David Platt, *Radical: Taking Back Your Faith from the American Dream* (New York: Multnomah, 2010).
3. Brandon Hatmaker, *Barefoot Church* (2011).
4. Avery Dulles, *Models of the Church,* expanded edition (New York: Random House, 1991).
5. Avery Dulles, *Models of the Church,* expanded edition (New York: Random House, 1991).
6. Abbe Francis Trochu, *The Cure D'Ars: St. Jean-Marie Baptiste Vianney.*
7. Avery Dulles, *Models of the Church,* expanded edition (New York: Random House, 1991).
8. Avery Dulles, *Models of the Church,* expanded edition (New York: Random House, 1991).
9. Lisa Lickona, *Magnificat Year of Mercy Companion* (New York: Magnificat, Inc., 2015).

Acknowledgments

This book, like countless others, could never have been completed without the assistance, guidance, influence, and support of so many people. Many of them don't even know that they've assisted with their friendship, their wisdom, and the examples of their lives.

First and foremost, I'm indebted to my wife, Teresa, who has had to listen to me prattle on year after year and then worked with me as I put my thoughts down on paper, revised, edited, chopped, rewrote, and edited again. For my daughter, Kristina, whose influence was priceless. For my sister, Regina, whose response was what I had hoped for but could never expect.

And then there was Fr. Rock Travnikar, my spiritual director for the last several years who encouraged me to write this book. Regretfully, I did not have his feedback, as God called him to heaven on Christmas of 2016, just days before we were to meet to review the latest manuscript. I pray that through his heavenly assistance the final work is more pleasing to him and to God.

For all those who were willing to provide feedback, especially Kathy, Ann, Carmen, Victor, Alexey, Rhonda, Fr. Kevin, Fr. David, Lawrence, and my dear Fr. Rock, may he rest in peace.

I am also indebted to my editor, Emily Gavigan. She encouraged me with her comments, improved the work considerably with her skills, talent, and hard work, and finally gave me confidence to move forward with the actual publishing.

For Ronald Deguzman, whose artistic skills captured the essence of my purpose with his rendering of Mother Teresa on the cover.

May God bless each of you and all those who I may have missed but are no less deserving of recognition and thanks.

Printed in the United States
By Bookmasters